NOTES FROM N
AND OTHER P

NOTES FROM NEW YORK

AND OTHER POEMS

Charles Tomlinson

Oxford   New York

OXFORD UNIVERSITY PRESS

1984

Oxford University Press, Walton Street, Oxford OX2 6DP

London Glasgow New York Toronto
Delhi Bombay Calcutta Madras Karachi
Kuala Lumpur Singapore Hong Kong Tokyo
Nairobi Dar es Salaam Cape Town
Melbourne Auckland

and associated companies in
Beirut Berlin Ibadan Mexico City Nicosia

Oxford is a trade mark of Oxford University Press

British Library Cataloguing in Publication Data
Tomlinson, Charles
Notes from New York and other poems.
I. Title
821'.914 PR 6039.O349
ISBN 0–19–211959–1

Library of Congress Cataloging in Publication Data
Tomlinson, Charles,—
Notes from New York and other poems.
I. Title
PR6039.O349N6 1984 821'.914 83–23661
ISBN 0–19–211959–1 (pbk.)

Printed in Great Britain by
J. W. Arrowsmith Ltd,
Bristol

To Brenda

ACKNOWLEDGEMENTS

ACKNOWLEDGEMENTS are due to the editors of the following: *The Christian Science Monitor, The Critical Quarterly, The London Magazine, The New Statesman, The Ontario Review, The Present Tense, Poetry Nation Review, The Times Literary Supplement, The Yale Literary Magazine, Vuelta* (Mexico). The following poems first appeared in *The Hudson Review*: 'Above Manhattan', 'History of a Malady', 'At the Trade Center', 'All Afternoon', 'In Verdi Square', 'Byzantium'.

I must also thank the editors of the BBC's 'Poetry Now' who first broadcast three of these poems.

CONTENTS

THE LANDING

Banking to land, as readily as birds
   We tilt down in. Manhattan
Beyond us is holding on to the rays
   Of a tawny strip of sun of late afternoon,
That catches on spire and pinnacle and then
   Shafts out the island entire:
A blaze across the Verrazano Narrows
   Conflagrates suburbs, the Jersey woods, and we
In our circling the only ones to see
   The total and spreading scope of it,
The Passaic flowing with fire towards the sun
   Just when one thinks the sundown over and done:
Scaling the silhouettes above the water
   In the eyries of the town the lights come on.

ABOVE MANHATTAN

Up in the air
among the Iroquois: no:
they are not born
with a head for heights:
their girder-going
is a learned, at last
a learnèd thing
as sure as instinct:
beneath them
they can see in print
the newssheet of the city
with a single rent where three
columns, clipped out of it,
show the Park was planted:
webbed and cradled
by the catenary
distances of bridge on bridge
the place is as real
as something imaginary:
but from where they are
one must read with care:
for to put
one foot wrong
is to drop
more than a glance
and though
this closeness and that distance
make dancing difficult a dance
it is that the mind is led
above Manhattan

Note: The Iroquois are employed in high construction work.

AT THE TRADE CENTER

Paused at the more than Brocken summit,
  Hand outstretched to touch and cover
The falling height beneath, I watch
  Between the nakedness of fingers—light
On each knuckled promontory of flesh
  And shadows tremulous between the gaps—
The map of land, the map of air:
  Rivers both sides of this island
Tug the gaze askance from the grid of streets
  To the sea- and bird-ways, the expanse
That drinks the reverberation of these energies.
  What can a hand bring back into a view
No rule of thumb made possible? It spans
  The given rigours and the generous remissions
Of ocean, of the ferryings to-and-fro
  Between the harbour and the islands. As you climb
The more you see of waters and of marsh
  Where, angle-poised, the heron
Stands within earshot of this city
  Back to the horizon, studying its pool.
The horizon is where we are:
  The Bridge is small from this new vantage,
The view in space become a view in time:
  Climbing we see an older city's fall—
The waterfront is down: the clerks are hived
  Window on window where the town began   ·
And spread. I spread my fingers
  And the traffic runs between. The elevator grounds
Us back to streets where in the cracks
  Between immeasurable buildings beggars
From their domains of dust and paper-bags
  Hold out one hand deep in the traffic sounds.

ON MADISON

We walk up Madison. It is the end
   Of a winter afternoon: the mist
Has cancelled out the reaches of the vista
   As the rivers (we cannot see them)
Assert their right to the island they enclose.
   So much of the surrounding, the unseen—
The homelessness beyond the mist-lopped towers—
   Presses upon us at this hour:
We savour the wine of the solitude of spaces
   In the same instant as we choose the street
That seems like a home returned to, grown
   Suddenly festive as we enter it
With the odour of chestnuts on the corner braziers.

WHAT VIRGINIA SAID

I like the crush here
we were standing by the stair
trying to insert our bodies
into the upward flow
out of the Liberty Express
I mean after that college town
I like that too
we were getting through now
But in a crowd you
always feel safe
especially at night
which is not true there
and were climbing
and were half-way
to the upper floors—
the drunks, the sleepy
addicts, the derelicts
outside the doors
of Penn Station
and she swimming on
ahead with a retrospective
laugh and one
hand waving *See you see you*
feeling safe

CROSSING BROOKLYN FERRY

To cross a ferry that is no longer there,
The eye must pilot you to the farther shore:
It travels the distance instantaneously
And time also: the stakes that you can see
Raggedly jettying into nothingness
Are the ghosts of Whitman's ferry: their images
Crowding the enfilade of steel and stone
Have the whole East River to reflect upon
And the tall solidities it liquefies.

IN VERDI SQUARE

A minute garden
you must not enter
and whose birds (there are notices)
you are forbidden to feed:

Verdi surveys it all
stone cloak on arm
as if about to quit
his pigeoned pedestal:

without coming down
he knows perfectly well
what operas are in town:
at the Ansonia Hotel

across the square
they have been practising
ever since Destinn and Caruso
and do so now:

ranged at his feet, stands
Falstaff beside
Aida and Leonora
watching a cast of thousands

pour into 72nd Street
as various as if the entire
complement of the complete
thirty operas were on stage at once

and crowding towards the green
silhouette of the Park
Olmsted had foreseen
against their advent, in '56—

the year *La Traviata*
arrived amid the brownstones and
vista on unfinished vista mapped
a half-empty island.

LAMENT FOR DOORMEN

In vestibules the doormen
shift red-headed pins
on the chart of rooms: these
figures in their landscape
are the ins and outs
abstracted to essences:
Mrs Schwamm has left for Tuba City
Mr Guglielmi has gone to his office
the Du Plessis are still sleeping
but the poetry of names
strikes little fire in the vestibule.
Spring: and the yellow cabs
go by each
with its Sun-King
inside and leave
doormen to their dark.
The lull of afternoon
brings them out under awnings
to rake the roadway for event
yawning into the quiet.
And you forget them
street on street of them
until a furtive movement
in the penumbra and
crossing the floor
of the confine ahead of you
one of them has the elevator
door open for your ascent.

ALL AFTERNOON

All afternoon the shadows have been building
A city of their own within the streets,
Carefully correcting the perspectives
With dark diagonals, and paring back
Sidewalks into catwalks, strips of bright
Companionways, as if it were a ship
This counter-city. But the leaning, black
Enjambements like ladders for assault
Scale the façades and tie them to the earth,
Confounding fire-escapes already meshed
In slatted ambiguities. You touch
The sliding shapes to find which place is which
And grime a finger with the ash of time
That blows through both, the shadow in the shade
And in the light, that scours each thoroughfare
To pit the walls, rise out of yard and stairwell
And tarnish the Chrysler's Aztec pinnacle.

THE ARRIVAL

Sailing at dawn into the Narrows,
The cliffs once passed and, level with the spokes
Of light that radiate the streets, we veer
At the edge of this great solar wheel
Whose axis buildings hide: here beam on beam
Haloes the place once more with all the hopes
Time has renewed in it, lost and recovered
Where expectation shrinks to a single yard,
A concourse of four gables round one tree
Straggling towards its sun, as ships unseen
Sway into their anchorage raying back
The incandescence of beginning day.

BYZANTIUM

In that 'corridor of garments'
Orchard Street the cry
of a gigantic nightingale or thrush
drops out of the sky.

Out of the sky?
Out of the water-whistle
of a vendor of plastic birds—
and with so much of pastoral artifice

that the Sundaying Jews
in their cars on
Delancey Street might be
tourists along the Vale of Hebron.

I choose a bird all green
for the colour that is not here
to testify to the birds of Gloucestershire
where it is I have been.

For, once I have gone
back, such a roulade
and cataract will never come
to the ear as on the sidewalks of Byzantium.

THE MIRROR IN THE ROADWAY

Nature here
is the multiplicity of luck
such as furniture in the street
when a mirror
hoisting the image
of a stopped truck
on to a dresser top
encloses its mass
inside the glass square
bevelled at the lip:
the mirror
has sheered away
all save the rear view—
a cargo of chairs, a piece
to be inserted elsewhere
in the jigsaw as the truck
moves off and leaves this high
fragment of deserted space
for the street to stare into
and where the chairs had hung
people it with the reflections of passers-by

HERO SANDWICHES

for John

Tuesday and Friday
are Hero Sandwich Day:
all other days
heroes must feed
on sandwiches
for the common breed of men
not these
vast open
energy-providers
Siegfried in search
of dragons or a bride
might breakfast on:
why do you never make
Hero Sandwiches
other days of the week
I ask the man
at the Delicatessen:
all he replies is
Tuesdays and Fridays
are our Blue Collar Special:
one cannot confute
logic so ready and so resolute:
clearly one must wait until
Blue Collar Special Day
arrives decreeing that
heroes in overalls
heroes in canticles
Whitman might have written
shall be provendered and provided
for their journey down-
stream with the Rhine
of the lunch-hour traffic
flowing through mid-town

OF THE WINTER BALL GAME

for Bill Humphrey

Of the winter ball game—
not that I could follow the play
and given my inability to
recognise until half-way through
which team was 'ours'—I must
say there was enough incidental
counterpoint to set
those Mars-men with padded shoulders
and the haphazard choreography of majorette
on majorette into one
seamless music as when
a black dog
suddenly crossed the pitch
as confused as I was
and out of a desolate sky
the sun appeared (just once)
and lit up the whole stadium
and everyone cheered to see
nature participate: the band
was playing I've got plenty of nothing and
nothing's plenty for me: something
kept dragging the day from focus—
the cold mostly that reddened
the bare legs of the cheer-leaders
and made them dance the harder:
it drove us home before
we knew what the score was: the event
our desertion excepted was a draw
between persistence and winter

ICE CREAM AT BLAUENBERG

The restaurant serving Char-Broiled Meats
Flavored in Flame, Welsh Farms Ice Cream,
Stands at a four-way stop between
A Dutch cemetery and an antique shop.

Eating our purchase in the scent of char-broil,
We read the tombs—all one great clan
It seems, named Voorhees or Van Zandt,
Inherit beneath these cenotaphs Jersey soil.

A dog without dignity or character
Of any sort comes cringing up to beg us
For whatever surplus overflows our cones,
All eyes, all blandishments, all shamelessness.

The sun is autumnal, but it melts our ices,
The stone is durable and free from moss,
Father, Mother, Our Parents, the lettering says:
They are buried without the drama of a cross

Which would seem, perhaps, presumptuous on this hill—
Even the crowning urns suggest they'd be
Useful if only you could reach them down
Out of the blue of this American day.

The urns are immovable whites and greys,
The ices keep running down our fingers,
Our cones are sticky—they were overfilled—
The dog with the sweet tooth sidles still and lingers.

Our aim had been the house named Rockingham
Washington lived in—in my mind's eye
I caught him at supper there, his campaigns done
Pictured him (painted by Leutze) Crossing the Delaware.

However, a wrong road was to bring us out
To the hush of these Dutchmen and this dog:
We give it the butts of our cones and the slush that's left,
Get back inside the car and turn about

Into the current of history going on,
Past the antique shop, then cutting back
Counter to the route the armies followed,
In the Sunday traffic and the shortening sun.

FROM THE MOTORWAY

Gulls flock in to feed from the waste
  They are dumping, truck by truck,
Onto a hump of land three roads
  Have severed from all other:
Once the seeds drift down and net together
  This shifting compost where the gulls
Are scavenging a winter living,
  It will grow into a hill—for hawks
A hunting ground, but never to be named:
  No one will ever go there. How
Shall we have it back, a belonging shape?
  For it will breed no ghosts
But only—under the dip and survey
  Of hawk-wings—the bones of tiny prey,
Its sodium glow on winter evenings
  As inaccessible as Eden . . .

TO IVOR GURNEY

Driving north, I catch the hillshapes, Gurney,
  Whose drops and rises—Cotswold and Malvern
In their cantilena above the plains—
  Sustained your melody: your melody sustains
Them, now—Edens that lay
  Either side of this interminable roadway.
You would recognise them still, but the lanes
  Of lights that fill the lowlands, brim
To the Severn and glow into the heights.
  You can regain the gate: the angel with the sword
Illuminates the paths to let you see
  That night is never to be restored
To Eden and England spangled in bright chains.

THE QUESTION

The curve of lamps that climbs into the dark
   And distances of moorland, leads-on the road
Past where the excavation first laid bare
   Secretive farms: our beams explore them there—
Gaunt hill-top shapes, slab-roofed
   And dour, although their panes give back
The festive scintillation of our lights. Within,
   The televisions fade and waver, their images
Unseamed by the unending cavalcade
   To north and south. When no-one came,
Was silence as oppressive as our sounds?
   We could scarcely be welcome here: and yet
May not time have so habituated them
   To all the accumulated shifts and strangenesses
That none can any longer feel what change
   Those resonant rooms have brought into their lives
Eased into sleep now by incessant wheels?

BLACK BROOK

Black Brook is brown. It travels
   With the hillside in it—an upside-down
Horizon above a brackened slope—until
   It drops and then: rags and a rush of foam
Whiten the peat-stained stream
   That keeps changing note and singing
The song of its shingle, its shallowness or its falls.
   I pace a parallel track to that of the water:
It must be the light of a moorland winter
   Let them say that black was fair name
For such a stream, making it mirror
   Solely the granite and the grey
As no doubt it can. But look! Black Brook
   Has its horizon back, and a blue
Inverted sky dyeing it through to a bed
   Of dazzling sand, an ore of gravel
It has washed out beneath rock and rowan
   As it came here homing down
To the valley it brightens belying its name.

POEM FOR MY FATHER

I bring to countryside my father's sense
Of an exile ended when he fished his way
Along the stained canal and out between
The first farms, the uninterrupted green,
To find once more the Suffolk he had known
Before the Somme. Yet there was not one tree
Unconscious of that name and aftermath
Nor is there now. For everything we see
Teaches the time that we are living in,
Whose piecemeal speech the vocables of Eden
Pace in reminder of the full perfection,
As oaks above these waters keep their gold
Against the autumn long past other trees
Poised between paradise and history.

THE JOURNEY

The sun had not gone down. The new moon
   Rose alongside us, set out as we did:
Grateful for this bright companionship
   We watched the blade grow sharp against the night
And disappear each time we dipped:
   A sliver of illumination at the crest
Awaited us, a swift interrogation
   Showed us the shapes we drove towards
And lost them to the intervening folds
   As our way descended. It was now
The travelling crescent suddenly began
   To leap from side to side, surprising us
At every fresh appearance, unpredictably
   Caught among the sticks of some right-hand tree
Or sailing left over roof and ridge
   To mock us. I know the explanation
But explanations are less compelling than
   These various returns and the expectancy that can
Never quite foresee the way
   The looked-for will look back at us
Across the deviousness of distances that keep on
   Lapsing and renewing themselves under a leaping moon.

THE ARCH

Good at maps and vistas, poor
At the varieties of grass and flower,
A car has at all events this to be said in its favour:
It has an eye for metamorphosis—
As when the windscreen frames the image
Of one of those tree-roofs arching the road
All apparent mass and solidity
Until you swing in under and fragments
(Or so the glance would say) start
Falling away and let the sky show
As you are passing beneath, staring up into
A shattered canopy, a leaf-floor
Swaying apart. The past
Receding into the tunnel mouth
That has instantly re-formed behind you,
Ledge on ledge of green masonry where you have gone
Flows back into place to close
Finally round an immovable keystone.

HEDGEROWS

for Peter Porter

In Suffolk they are no longer there:
   The post-modern landscape has gone medieval:
The stuff for the staff of life you townsmen
   Still lean on, Peter, flows up to the tarmac
An inland sea. Once they begin to disappear
   You see what an urbanity hedgerows are:
Feeling their way across the featureless land,
   Shutting out swamp and gripping the soil together,
They contain, compel as civilly as stanzas
   In the cultivator's poem of earth and sun
Where harvests fatten to be freighted up for London.

THE SHOUT

Somebody's shout displaces the horizon:
   Distance rushes at foreground things
Like a flare of lengthening light
   And tears at one's steps with the sound of the shout.
It was in play no doubt, but whoever raised it
   Has gone on unaware of the way the air
Roused and rippled outwards to give it space.
   Besides me, the rooks have taken it in,
Rising and wheeling in a blank sky
   On which the early dark is stiffening
Its silhouettes at the reverberations of that cry.

HIGH SUMMER

Buzzards bring out their young one
  Circling, show it the map of woods,
The fields of prey, drive at it
  Diving it downwards and away, then
Let it rise to take up space
  Under its wings, their incessantly insisting
Note teaching it what kingdom
  It is the prince of, crying it awake to things:
They lead it aloft now feeling
  The currents pull through emptiness—emptiness
That is full of the invitation to height and flight—,
  Through blue where only a combed-out floss
Presaging fair weather faintly clouds
  The zenith they are climbing. Down that height
The currents tremor earthwards, tug
  And turn up the undersides of leaves
Into the light until they give it back
  As if from a turning of those wings
One can no longer see: the two
  High Aztec messengers of the sun
Telling over and over the sources of blood
  Hang dark and far against the upper blue
Pulsating beside their studious progeny.

THE QUARRY

The gap where the quarry is keeps moving away,
    As each year they cut and fill
The hillside, draw out its veins
    Of stone until the cranes are ready
To lift them in severed lengths
    Leaving the rifts behind—and soon
They, too, disappear. The house
    That clung to the brink is sailing back
On a tide of green. One day it will be
    Out of sight of all this activity and dust,
And the gap itself finally close,
    When a field, whose hedge no longer greys
To the tone of the stone-meal, has covered it,
    And other eyes in travelling this way
Will feel the difference an appraise it then.

THE BEECH

Blizzards have brought down the beech tree
   That, through twenty years, had served
As landmark or as limit to our walk:
   We sat among its roots when buds
Fruitlike in their profusion tipped the twigs—
   A galaxy of black against a sky that soon
Leaf-layers would shut back. The naked tree
   Commanded, manned the space before it
And beyond, dark lightnings of its branches
   Played above the winter desolation:
It seemed their charge had set the grass alight
   As a low sun shot its fire into the valley
Splitting the shadows open. Today that sun
   Shows you the place uncitadelled,
A wrecked town centred by no spire,
   Scattered and splintered wide. At night
As the wind comes feeling for those boughs
   There is nothing now in the dark of an answering strength,
No form to confront and to attest
   The amplitude of dawning spaces as when
The tower rebuilt itself out of the mist each morning.

AFTER THE STORM

Waters come welling into this valley
  From a hundred sources. Some
Sealed by the August heat, dry back
  From a dusty bed and only when the leaves
Are down again, rustle and rush
  In their teeming gulley after the storm.
Today—just once—the sun looks forth
  To catch the misty emanations of our north
Rising in spirals underneath the hill:
  Here, like a steaming beast, a house
Emerges into its beams, the mist
  Smoking along them into a vapour veil
That trails up into soaked branches
  Sending down shower on shower.
The sky is clear for an hour. Where the sun
  Is going under it seems to impose
That silence against which the streams keep telling
  Over and over in the ebbing light
In their voices of liquid suasion, of travelling thunder
  From what depths they have drunk and from what heights.

CONFLUENCE

Where the hillside stream unearths itself
   You can catch nothing but its urgent voice
Laying claim to the air and bearing down
   On all that lies below. Then, finding
A bed to flow into, submitting
   To go the way a valley goes, it silences.
The mind goes with the water feeling free,
   Yields itself to the sea's gravity.
Following downhill I no longer hear
   The querulousness of the emerging spring:
New the sound that fills the mind's ear now,
   Each vein and voice of the watershed
Calling to the estuary as they near,
   Tuning themselves to the slopes and stones
They flow across: the weirs and the thresholds
   Of the bridges cleared, a singleness
Out of all the confluences pours on
   To a music of what shapes, what stays and passes
Between this island and its seas,
   Off sandstone, moorslope, shales and scarp
Creation overleaping its seven days.

IN DECEMBER

The fog, as it enters the lowland, is smoothing away
   All demarcations, transforming into a bay
Of white and level waters the valley mouth:
   The tide keeps running and rising
Until it fills from side to side
   The whole of the space before us and its cold
Is on our faces now. This grey lava,
   Gliding apocalypse undoes the promise
Of the bay it has hardly formed,
   Climbs like water coming to a level
It cannot find until it closes
   The narrowing parallel between the skyline
And itself: a house goes down
   Into an underwater world, a core
Of warmth in the sea that minutes since
   Was merely a shore. But in this play
Of the last or is it the first day
   By midnight the sky is clear: no sign
Of what has passed save in the transformation
   Of mist to the drops that star the grass:
The horizon is keeping its distance and its nearness
   Between the glittering of earth and galaxies,
Worlds within worlds encircling our walls
   From the recesses and recessions of winter skies.

AT A GLANCE

The mountains, from this downward turn in the road,
  Are sometimes there of a morning, sometimes gone:
Today, you could almost rest your hand upon
  Their bulky ripple and feel it
Flow out like paint at a brush-tip,
  Feel also the exact resistance of that flow:
It is an abyss one looks across—
  Whole tracts and counties melted in a glance
That, meeting the sky-line limit,
  Turns it into a nearness as if such
Ease of the sight were in possession of the touch.
  And so it is. Light touches the sense awake,
First fiat crossing the aeons to an eye
  That sees it is still good, its touch a healing
Where yesterday revealed at this turn of the hill
  Only a void and formlessness of sky.

THE GLACIER

We climbed that day
Up into a region where the mist
Stagnated over beds of slate—a waste
Of mountain ground we had approached
Through grass and moss, themselves as grey
As the accumulating dust (for it was summer)
That soiled the trickling glacier where it lay.
Over the blackened razors of the slate
Crumbling as they cut, we slithered by
One eye upon the blades beneath our feet,
One searching the source that fed a slow
Continuous water out of ice and snow
Into this carious mass. That source
Contouring round the mountain's form
Coiled along the ledges with a hold
Slackened by thaw, then frozen firm by cold—
The glacier's edge, eating at the track
That faltered past it. We trusted that faint line
To take us back and down, and so it did:
The glacier, overshadowing our minds,
In a sordid glistening outwaited our descent
To where the final macerations, siftings
Of moraines staining the torrents brown,
Had turned, at last, to the soil which fructifies
In the plains a wide and level shore.

NIGHT FISHERS

After the autumn storms, we chose a night
   To fish the bay. The catch
I scarcely recollect. It was the climb,
   The grasp at slipping rock unnerved
All thought, thrust out of time
   And into now the sharp original fear
That mastered me then. I do not think
   I ever looked so far down into space
As through the clefts we over-leapt:
   Beams of our torches given back
Off walls and water in each rift
   Crossed and recrossed one another, so the mind
Recalling them, still seems to move
   Inside a hollow diamond that the dark
As shadows shift, threatens to unfacet:
   It was no jewel, it was the flesh would shatter.
And yet it did not. Somehow we arrived
   And crouched there in the cool. The night
Save for the whispered water under-cliff,
   The hiss of falling casts, lay round
Thick with silence. It seemed
   A sky spread out beneath us, constellations
Swimming into view wherever fish
   Lit up its dark with phosphor. A thousand
Points of light mapped the expanse
   And depth, and yet the cliff-top height
Hinted no pull of vertigo along
   Its sudden edge: through diaphanous waters
The radium in the flowing pitchblende glowed
   Holding both mind and eye
Encompassed by a stir of scattered lambency:
   And unalarmed, I could forget
As night-bound we fished on unharmed,
   The terrors of the way we'd come, put by
The terrors of return past fault and fall,
   Watching this calm firmament of the sea.

NEAR HARTLAND

We came by night,
  Drove the great avenue of beech
—A mile of them—in a dark
  That lopped their summits. Dead they seemed
To the glare that raked the boughless trunks
  Lichened, spare. Daylight restored
Their foliage: each westerly tree
  Taking its inclination from the sea-wind
East, had knit with its neighbour opposite
  A straining arch above the roadway.
We left through the colonnade we came by
  And watched above us the Atlantic breathe and pile
Its airy tonnage down that aisle of branches
  Trying the roof-ties between side and side:
Like travellers in the maelstrom's eye
  We rode closed in a ring of force
That flowed from roots to tree-tip,
  Coiled back to carry and withstand
The long swell out of Labrador
  Pouring across this heaving mile of England.

MORWENNA'S CLIFF

The glance drops here like a hawk falling,
   Grasps, from above, the tide-edge
Gliding in and shaping itself to a profile,
   To a certainty of nose, full lips and chin:
The face comes imaging up from chaos
   Just where the bedrock forces water
To an instant of definition, lost
   Till the next wave meets with white
The same resistance. Hawks hang
   And the fine bones bleach where conies
Lurk in their warrened cliff, where only
   A man could trace out a human face
Printing and reprinting itself as the waters mass.

NEAR CEIBWR

The castle has gone into the cliff:
  These rocks that recall the origins of earth
Cannot remember it. Only the roots
  Of the bracken suspect the whereabouts
Of unguarded threshold stones. But they
  Are deaf to the searching whisper of the sea
That startles our ears with the very tone
  That flowed up to the sentry looking down.

AT THE HILL FORT

Walls, from its looted stones, defend
  Hayfields against the Irish Sea: today
More boisterous than belligerent a westerly
  Lifts and then lets fall as if in play
A flock of jackdaws that nest along the outcrop:
  They rise like chaff, hover like thistledown
Between a scooping-up and a droop, a drop.
  Hard to say which is at play with which
As they ride up the air yet again,
  A pattern, at first, of filings uncertainly
Magnetised together; toil and toy
  With the wind and let it tame them,
Flung back at their rock in alternations
  Of secure possession and a daring joy
In their world above walls within earshot of the sea.

THE MOMENT

Watching two surfers walk toward the tide,
Floating their boards beside them as the shore
Drops slowly off, and first the knee, then waist
Goes down into the elemental grasp,
I look to them to choose it, as the one
Wave gathers itself from thousands and comes on:
And they are ready for it facing round
Like birds that turn to levitate in wind:
All is assured now as they slide abreast:
Much as I envy them their bodies' skill
To steady and prolong the wild descent,
I choose that moment when their choice agrees
And, poised, they hesitate as though in air
To a culmination half theirs and half the sea's.

WRITING ON SAND

Birds' feet and baby feet,
Man Friday prints,
dog-pads
cramponned with claws,
ribbed shoe-soles—
hints there
of a refusal
to bare oneself
to the elemental,
a pacing parallel
to the incoming onrush, a
careful circuiting
of the rock pools:
the desire to stay
dry to be read
in the wet dust.
By what way
did that one
return?—he
of the stark striders,
the two perfect five-toed
concaves aimed
direct at the waves
whose own aim is
to remove
all clues
under the primeval slidings,
to erase them
to a swimming Braille,
an illegible Ogham,
to wash the slate clean.

VAN GOGH

I thought, once, that your hillshapes swam and swayed
Only in rhythm with that rising tide
Which mastered and unmade you at the last.
Yet if they did, there's this I judged awry:
It was such health you felt for in those hills
As madness robbed you of: your haste to fill
The no-man's land of space between the eye
And what it reached at, was a sanity,
For you abhorred both vacuum and dream:
It was not seeming, but solidities
That took your glance: it was a love of substance
Bound you to Arles. The apocalyptic night
Strained at the mysteries you could not see,
But sight asked to be fed, and chose for food
The daily bread of street, of room and bed.
The nebular revelations of the sky
Hovered and coiled, yet earth held till that day
When hills no longer pressed their bulwarks round
But shattered to echoes as if it were they had ceased.

LEGEND

The hill-top schloss
with its roots of stone
cellar on cellar
feels through and down

into the soil
the saecular dark
where space turns blind
and time is murk

from root to tower
an ascension seeks
for the lighted room
where someone sleeps

then walking goes
to the source of sun
the slit of a window
that gives out on

Bluebeard's domain
that will never
surrender space
to the torture chamber

to the clink of the treasury
the walled-in garden
the lake of tears
or the armourer's burden

in this kingdom's light
an undertone
shares the phosphorescence
of a pool in limestone

that cupped by the rock
of the underground
spreads opaque and thick
to its glinting bound

and this is well
for the deep and the high
riding horizons
replenish the eye

with all that terrain
it cannot see
on which it must raise
the hive and immensity

of a hill-top schloss
with roots of stone
cellar on cellar
feeling through and down

THE SOUND OF TIME

When the clock-tick fades
out of the ear
you can listen to time
in the flow of fire:

and there a cascade
streams up the coals:
loud as Niagara
these climbing falls:

it pours within
forked and fleering
over the thresholds
of a deafened hearing

till the superfluity
of the room's recess
has filled the auricle
with time's abyss

HISTORY OF A MALADY

Plangebant aliae proceris tympana palmis—Catullus

I

'Others beat timbrels with uplifted hands':
    Across the words a ripple drifted
As if the onomatopoeia had excited
    The eyes themselves, fluttering a pulse in them:
But what, as it guttered and renewed,
    The ripple did was wake one to that pitch
The body had reached already: the same
    Thing would have chanced without the words:
For had I been outside, a ripple
    Would have travelled across the distances
Drawing a comet-train behind it,
    The patterned flashes sparking to a pulse
Till the whole field of sight
    Blossomed corollas of disintegrating rays:
We live at the surface of our bodies
    With only the pain to tell the presence there
Of a history whose pressure we ignored:
    To follow out that history from its source
One would have needed to retreat
    Turning away from life and listening
Only to the roar of blood. Today
    As the migraine fluttered and then burst
In a swarm of lights, I knew the body
    Had been travelling in darkness and for days
Towards this consummation in confusion
    When the body's quiet and its spongey dark
Wince with neon gleams, a corridor
    In the invaded citadel where messengers
Arrive with excited and uncertain news,
    With memory, beset by malady, of when
The unquestioning mind inhabited its flesh
    And, moving in time and rhyme with the body's ease,
We beat the timbrels with uplifted hands.

II

Not Dostoievsky's fit and fall: gentler
    Than that: yet with a violence of its own:
A velocity of the cells seizes the mind,
    The speed of this flare on flare

Taking pace from the recurring nightmare
  Of a week of dreams, the hurtling journey
Nowhere that, waking, one forgot. This dislocation
  Between sleep and seeing, what did it mean
Save that the body had made off alone
  Blind to direction—that one lacked by day
A measure of its urgency? Times are
  When a superabundance of the senses
Preludes this familiar disarray. Why
  Does one take no warning then
From their elation? It has occurred before
  And one should know it: unknowing
Breeds another dislocation: this time
  Body has not gone off alone—
One has gone with it exulting in its tone
  And capabilities: the eye exults also
Finding all colours prime—the humid
  Blues, the greys of dust. Forms
Now are all that they should be: a tree
  With its shock of foliage sways
Precise as the flower-head of a rose,
  As undeclared, too—move the glance
An inch and there is so much that is new
  To be read in that unpossessable shape
That could be said now with a perfect adequacy
  Or so it seems. But one took warning
Neither from dreams nor this. One should have entered
  Suspiciously this Eden of the sight
As one attends to the brittle brightness
  That on a day of spring spells rain:
Instead, sharpness turns its edge
  As the first distorting ripple
Starts to spread and first lights
  Flare the eye, powering it to the pulse
Of rapped and clinking tambourines Catullus
  Heard and trapped beating into the words.

III

Beating into the words?
Verse does not know
where malady becomes melody
nor can rehearse:

55

this is the gift
I did not bargain for:
I would not choose it
nor can I refuse:

circling and dancing
so it seems—
despite the double
violence of dreams and light:

this is the angel with the sword
the shining double-bladed word
a lingering at the gate
of Eden late or early.

DESERT AUTUMN

Dead grasshoppers'
bone-white
hollow shells
swirl with the dry
leaves in the ditch:
a month since
they—flat eye,
thin legs—
shone with a lustre
dust could not
utterly tarnish,
striped black
striped brown
like the beadwork
Indian hands
had patterned:
weeds and sand
are the world
they sprang through
and the leathery stalks,
sun-flowers,
poor corn, all
faded yellow
like grasshoppers' wings
still kept then the bright
green of spring as they
first leapt into sunlight.

MICTLANTECUHTLI

I saw past the door, today,
into the death god's palace:
it was a look, no more,
a place of snow and ice:

as the plane rose up
it was then I saw it
high over the valley and
at the volcano's summit:

a crater of blown snows,
snow caught in each fold
where the lava paths led
from the drifted threshold:

the accurate Aztecs
carved the skull god's device
out of rock crystal
as transparent as ice:

when the conquerors climbed
from the heat to his doorway
his icicle fence they brought
dripping back to the valley:

yet out of the whole vast
melted hierarchy
one sole god has lasted
and that is he

AT TROTSKY'S HOUSE

A barrel-organ
assails the suburb
with *Tales from the Vienna Woods*:
in Calle Viena
the garden is guarded
by wall and turret
and an aleatory score
of bullet holes
pocks the interior.
Lev Davidovich slept here
and this is the table
at which he wrote,
the goatee shedding its stray hairs
over the books, the pamphlets.
Words, words . . . there are cylinders
for the silent dictaphone
and a bottle of Waterman's Ink long dry.
And this is the way he
left things
the day of the assassination?
Más o menos, sí.
He is courteous in three languages
the great man's grandson—
Does he never return to Europe?
De temps en temps.
Under the palm outside
whose rind is peeling,
Europe, or one's own part of it,
seems a distant planet:
and the Moscow
to which the urn of ashes
is awaiting its return
lies kremlined forever in historic snow.

LOS POBRECITOS

Caridad para los pobrecitos
she is saying, her hand
outstretched as she
sways towards me:
diminutives sweeten
between beggar and giver
the injustices of living:
hers is a courteous race
accustomed to endure:
gentle and cunning is what they are
these sitters in shadows,
dogging the porches where
they are both prologue and epilogue
to each gold interior.

TEOTIHUACÁN

Compra? compra?—the street cry
of the pyramids:
will you buy? will you buy?
It is the gods they are selling.
The girl with her *idolitos*
offers us *La Diosa de la Muerte*
—*Genuine*, she adds.
                                    Genuine
comes echoing back
the whole way up this pyramid:
it seems to be inhabited
by a priesthood of vendors,
each one
vouching for the authenticity
of his own particular god.
Now the gods are dead
their houses greet a sky
freed of their weight
and from a summit that is a plain
the flat-topped pyramids repeat
the volcanic horizons of this high terrain
that cone on cone
opens its fastnesses to a mythless sun.

VALLE DE OAXACA

for Roberto Donis

Trumpeters
from the Comandancia militar
in the last glare of day
are practising a fanfare:

their notes float off
buffeted by walls
into a shower of chromatics
that falls round the ears of the women at the washing trough:

a celebration? You might call it that
as it harmonises with the tones
that toll from Santo Domingo—
a celebration, but of what?

Oh it's a desultory enough affair
I know: perhaps little more
than that the sun is shining
and they are standing where they are

under a tree's wide shade
where they've begun
to lay their instruments down
as they cross to the other side

of the barrack yard
to join the talkers there,
easy as unhurried men should be
conversing in the cooling air:

the abandoned instruments
gleam on, a heap
the low sun grazes
tracing the glinting contours of a sleep

tomorrow's dawn will scatter as
trumpeters set lips to brass
to waken also us as they
shake down reveilleing echoes over town and valley

Flying south-west—say Washington to Albuquerque—unlulled by printed matter, stoical at the colour and taste of airline food, one can see things that were once only imagined.

I like that moment when, as the plane rises, its shadow shrinks smaller and smaller, until it looks like an accompanying black bird down there. Then it gets lost in the mathematic of the suburbs, as the first clouds drift past and one climbs through them to emerge high above their flocculent plain. They become one's horizon now. In doing so, they intensify for one that sense of things always moving, disintegrating, re-forming—the sense of a world which is never quite *there* because light and time have changed it. The clouds are no longer exactly a plain: they are cloud herds, cloud flocks, cloud islands, floes packing a seascape, and below that extend the map-lines of an undersea land whose houses are dotting a sea-floor.

Over Dakota a cloudy vagueness mists the squared-off fields, as though a colourless sandstorm were streaming across them. There is an odd pathos about the patchwork quiet of the mapped-out land, as if someone had undertaken to measure accurately this immeasurable continent, only to be frustrated by the encroaching of mountain-masses, lakeshapes, rivercourses, saltflats, the humping and wrinkling of the terrain countering the human insistence on angles and straight lines.

Sight becomes a double mystery up here, because so frequently one cannot make out what precisely it is that one is looking at. Again, this merely intensifies a daily experience. Indeed, before embarking, and while driving into the airport this morning, I caught sight of what seemed to be an injured gull struggling on the tarmac: a second later, beaked, bent and rocking in the wind, it resolved itself into a scrap of twisted paper. In flight, we climb above hill-folds, then mountains: a white smoke over their highest point solidifies into snow hooding a peak. It is an exact replica of snow until the eye distinguishes a faint movement in it: cloud! It is the perfect cloak to this mountain inaccessibility, closing off one of the Bible's 'high places', a sierra Sinai, under the purest fleece.

Sight and flight: we are flying and so is the day. Sunset lies along the edge of our cloud horizon, flushing it a deeper royal purple, holding to the west in an orange stripe just ahead of the darkening cloud-edge. Behind us all is black. We fly towards that sunset where it is transfusing cloud-stuff with its orange fire while beneath us the clouds spread opaquely ocean-like, sliding back in even waves into the darkness. A sunset, enduring beyond the normal event, draws us westward, a nocturne in four bands of ascending colours, blue, yellow, orange, black, striped like a Mexican blanket. It glows on out of the dusk, retreating while we manage to keep it just in sight. Like the angles and lines of fields and roads across the landscape, the plane, in its westward trajectory, seems to partake of that same desire to bring the universe under the rule of measure. It will abolish space, or at least shrink it, and it will defy time as it chases the sunset—that sunset which remains so tantalisingly how many hundred miles ahead, securely eluding us.

In this world which is never quite there, because the light has passed on, and 'everything flows', the plane lifts us across a continent and will soon deposit us among the ordinary demands of our lives. The Sinai peak lies behind us now, along with the sky-seas and the cloud-continents. But they persist to haunt the mind, rising sheer beyond us, not mocking us, but reassessing us, not so much scaling us down as redefining for us that universe of which we too are a part.